Original title:
Oakwood Echoes

Copyright © 2025 Creative Arts Management OÜ
All rights reserved.

Author: Ryan Sterling
ISBN HARDBACK: 978-1-80566-789-6
ISBN PAPERBACK: 978-1-80566-809-1

## In the Wake of Autumn's Hand

Squirrels prance on branches high,
Chasing leaves that twist and fly.
Acorns bounce like little balls,
Nature's jest, it giggles and stalls.

The colors clash, a wild parade,
Fallen leaves, a leafy cascade.
The air is crisp, the wind is sly,
As pumpkins roll and giggle nearby.

## Pathways of Mystique and Leaf Fall

Wandering paths where shadows play,
Where whispers tease and fates sway.
Every step, a crunch with glee,
An orchestra of leaves, carefree.

A fox winks with mischief bright,
Dodging Dale and his flighty kite.
What's that sound? A bubbling brook!
Or maybe it's just the pranking rook!

## Underneath the Canopy of Time

Branches wave like silly hands,
Tickling the sky, forming bands.
Sunlight laughs as it plays tag,
Amongst the trunks, they dance and wag.

Hours drift, like butterflies,
As shadows giggle and tease the skies.
Each rustle brings a cheerful tune,
Nature's jest, a merry swoon.

## Dreams of Canopied Shadows

In the dusk, where the creatures creep,
The owls hoot, and the shadows leap.
A raccoon, with eyes so bright,
Steals a snack in the pale moonlight.

Dreamers wander with silly grins,
Catching whispers on leaf-lined winds.
As mischief brews beneath the trees,
Night giggles softly, with playful ease.

## Memories Carved in Bark

In the woods where creatures dwell,
Old trees giggle, stories they tell.
Squirrels plan their acorn heist,
While rabbits dance, not thinking twice.

Woodpeckers tap, the beat is bright,
A fox in boots claims it's all right.
The owls hoot, they roll their eyes,
As raccoons plot with snickered sighs.

## Secrets of the Woodland Spirits

Mossy feet and playful sprites,
Hide and seek in soft moonlight.
A fairy's sneeze gives all away,
Laughter echoes, come what may.

The bees gossip, buzzing loud,
While dainty deer prance, very proud.
A raccoon steals a picnic spread,
While squirrels feast upon their bread.

## A Dance with the Old Giants

Tall and mighty, roots so deep,
The old giants sway, they hardly sleep.
Branches waving, hats up high,
All join in when the winds sigh.

Breezes tickle, causing a stir,
A waltzing worm makes the crowd purr.
With each spin, laughter fills the air,
Though tree bark's stuck in a squirrel's hair!

**Twilight in the Leafy Realm**

As daylight fades, shadows creep,
The critters of dusk begin to leap.
A hedgehog in shades struts with flair,
While fireflies twinkle, glowing in the air.

Chasing tails in a playful race,
A nighttime feast, with much disgrace.
The moon's a witness to all that's weird,
In the leafy realm, no one has feared.

## **Nature's Silenced Anthem**

In the woods where whispers play,
Squirrels argue, come what may.
Trees shake leaves in funny glee,
Nature's choir, a silly spree.

Beneath a branch, a critter sleeps,
While the groundhog takes great leaps.
A frog croaks jokes in the sun,
Nature's laughter, never done.

## The Call of the Timeless

When the sun dips low and glows,
An ancient tree starts to propose.
With a wink, it shares a tale,
Of raccoons that once set sail.

Old bark remembers all the fun,
When mice wore hats and squirrels could run.
The owl hoots, 'Come join the dance!'
In this forest, all get a chance.

## Guardians of the Green

Sturdy trunks with grins so wide,
Guard the secrets where creatures hide.
A rabbit juggles seeds and nuts,
While hedgehogs giggle, 'What a guts!'

In the evening, shadows creep,
While the chipmunks spin and leap.
Every root tells a funny tale,
In this realm, laughter prevails.

## Spirits in the Timber

The spirits dance 'neath moonlit skies,
Tickling leaves and closing eyes.
With every breeze, a chuckle swells,
As fireflies share their buzzing spells.

Among the brambles, shadows wink,
A band of ghosts begins to think.
'We miss the days of silly pranks,
And squirrels' acrobatic thanks.'

## Remembering Whispers in the Air

A squirrel danced on a twig,
Wobbly like a hot-air pig.
It chattered loud, all out of tune,
Claiming to be the best raccoon.

The leaves giggled, rustled light,
As the sun began its flight.
A rabbit hopped, tripped on a word,
His friends rolled their eyes, absurd!

## Nature's Soft Serenade of Solitude

The breeze hummed, a silly tune,
Tickling noses, making them swoon.
A toad croaked its best opera hit,
Leaving the crickets in sheer wit.

The branches waved, all in jest,
Joking with birds, 'Who's the best?'
A fox laughed, blushed in the shadows,
Saying, 'I'm the king of meadows!'

## Gifts of the Forest's Embrace

Beneath the boughs, a picnic laid,
With sandwich dreams, love's charade.
Ants marched in, an army so small,
Claiming crumbs, standing tall.

The mushrooms grinned, all in a row,
Whispering secrets of fun below.
A deer pranced, said, 'What a feast!'
Squirrels gasped, 'To the Mimic, at least!'

## Beyond the Whispering Wood

Behind the trees, a dance began,
Chaotic moves by a crazy man.
The owls blinked, amused, aghast,
While the fawns wondered how long it'd last.

The trails snickered, leaves would sway,
As laughter chased the dusk away.
A clever crow cawed, "Join the fun!"
For in the woods, we all are one!

## **When the Wind Speaks**

When the breeze takes a trip,
It whispers secrets all around,
Telling tales of squirrels' flips,
While the branches dance unbound.

A leaf falls with a silly plop,
And lands right on my head,
The trees start to sway and bop,
As if they're laughing instead.

## Embraced by the Grove

In shadows where the laughter rings,
The trees play hide and seek,
With branches that twist like joyful springs,
Their giggles never weak.

A toe stub here, a branch that sways,
The roots chuckle low and deep,
As I dodge their tricky maze,
They cradle me in playful sleep.

**Harmony in Green**

Frogs croak like they're singing stars,
While crickets tap a beat,
A dance-off under moonlit bars,
Where clovers form the seat.

And squirrels in tuxedos prance,
With acorns in their paws,
Inviting all to join the dance,
With nature's cheerful laws.

## Echoing Footsteps

Each step I take upon the trail,
Leaves giggle and clink,
They echo back a playful tale,
As if they're winking, I think!

A raccoon gives me quite a stare,
As if to say, 'What's new?'
I tip my hat, aware we share,
This forest rendezvous.

## Tales of Twisted Roots

Once a squirrel had a dream,
To wear a hat and drink some cream.
But as he danced on high up there,
He slipped and knocked down all his hair.

Beneath the branches, wise old crow,
Told knock-knock jokes to all below.
The laughter echoed, wild and bright,
As critters chuckled through the night.

A rabbit tried to impress a doe,
With fancy hops, a wild show.
But his landing was quite a flop,
And off he went, in a dizzy hop.

With tales of laughter filled with cheer,
In a forest where all gather near.
So grab your hat, let's start the fun,
This crazy life's for everyone!

## Symphony of the Sylvan Beings

In the glade, a concert started,
With frogs on leads, the wildlife charted.
Crickets played the fiddles with flair,
While fireflies danced in the cool night air.

The bears rolled drums, all paws and shake,
While raccoons served snacks, for goodness' sake.
An owl conducted, a wise old sage,
As nature's bands took center stage.

From acorns dropped like drumsticks bold,
They played their tunes with spirits untold.
A deer slipped on a banana peel,
And bumbled in with a funny squeal.

With every sound, the woods did cheer,
For this wild concert, it was clear,
That laughter echoed through the trees,
In harmony with the playful breeze.

## Time's Embrace in Green Halls

In halls of green where shadows play,
Time wobbles like a bowl of clay.
A hedgehog lost his watch one day,
And now he's late, hip-hip-hooray!

The wise old turtle took a stroll,
Claimed he'd race, but lost control.
He tripped on roots, fell with a thud,
Creating quite a muddy flood.

A playful breeze whispered secrets low,
As chipmunks giggled with their show.
They spun a tale of mischief grand,
While ants plotted their vast bandstand.

With laughter blooming in every nook,
Nature's whimsy lightly shook,
As moments twirled in jests so fine,
Crafting folly entwined with time.

## **Starlit Dreams among the Boughs**

Under boughs where stars unite,
Dreams are woven into the night.
A raccoon, dressed in a shiny suit,
Thought he'd lead a dance, how cute!

The owls hooted, keeping time,
To the rhythm of a tree's old rhyme.
A fox attempted the latest trends,
But ended up making silly bends.

Beneath the moon's soft, silvery gaze,
All creatures joined in playful praise.
With twinkling eyes and hearts so light,
They spun round 'til the dawn's first light.

In this starlit world, so full of glee,
Where laughter flows like the mighty sea,
Each dream a treasure, a friendly call,
For in this wonderland, there's joy for all.

## Songs of the Waiting Grove

In the grove where squirrels play,
They dance and chase their nuts away.
A crow sings tunes so off-key,
Even the trees begin to flee.

Beneath the leaves, a rabbit grins,
He plays the drums with acorn skins.
Every twig's a stage for fun,
Even the sun joins in the run.

A fox with flair strikes a pose,
While bees buzz sweetly in their clothes.
The mushrooms cheer for a chance to sing,
With each silly step, the forest swings.

Through laughter loud, the shadows curl,
Nature's stage, where dreams unfurl.
Here in the waiting grove we find,
Joyful antics, love intertwined.

## Beneath the Hearty Fronds

Beneath fronds wide, the critters feast,
On berries plump, they munch with least.
A raccoon juggles shiny things,
As laughter hums on little wings.

An owl's joke takes flight at night,
Making the stars burst with delight.
While fireflies wink with giddy glee,
They glow to the rhythm of jubilee.

The hedgehogs roll in grassy fray,
With wobbly spins, they steal the play.
While doves coo softly, hearts aglow,
In this laughter, time seems slow.

As night unfolds, all friends unite,
Beneath warm fronds, a sheer delight.
The forest echoes with their cheer,
In hearty banter, none disappear.

## Echoes of the Forest Heart

Beneath the boughs, the laughter swells,
Where stories spin like ringing bells.
A chipmunk tells a tale so grand,
It leaves the oaks in laughter spanned.

With every rustle in the trees,
A chorus of giggles rides the breeze.
The playful fox makes quite the scene,
Starring in antics, oh so keen.

An arborist's folly, he drops his map,
While ladybugs applaud, a joyful clap.
The forest whispers with a cheeky grin,
As acorns fall like chuckles win.

In the heart, where the whispers roam,
Echoes of mirth create a home.
Every creature, every spark,
In the joyful dance, they leave a mark.

## The Worn Path of Loyal Souls

On the path where friends convene,
With steps of laughter and shades of green.
A turtle trips, a stumble slight,
While rabbits giggle at the sight.

With whispered tales of silly pranks,
The trees join in with leafy thanks.
A raccoon wears a hat, oh dear,
The woodland critters clap and cheer.

A dance begins upon the road,
Each creature plays their silly code.
In squirrel leaps and hedgehog spins,
Loyal souls find joy in wins.

The worn path leads to endless fun,
With every step, the day is won.
In this realm of spirit whole,
Together we sing, heart and soul.

## Melodies of the Woodland Guardian

A squirrel sings a silly song,
His acorn hat just feels too strong.
The rabbits dance in twirling flops,
While hedgehogs join with tiny hops.

A fox strums notes on wooden strings,
While badgers boast of grander things.
The owl hoots out some offbeat shouts,
As all the forest laughs and pouts.

The trees sway lightly left and right,
As creatures gather, what a sight!
With every note, their troubles fade,
In nature's groove, their worries trade.

So if you hear a strangled cheer,
Just know the jester's drawing near.
In leafy realms, the laughter swells,
Where woodland magic always dwells.

## Through the Veil of Twilight's Kiss

At dusk the fireflies take their stand,
They won't lend light; they play in bands.
The crickets chirp a raucous dish,
A tune that grants the night a wish.

The moon sneezes low with a glimmer bright,
And raccoons debate if it's day or night.
A mouse in shades tries to dress just right,
Says, 'Fashion's tricky; can we take flight?'

Bats in capes fly like it's grand,
While coyotes howl, a strum of the band.
The wind whispers secrets, light and breezy,
As trees chuckle, feeling quite cheesy.

So lend an ear to the night's funny show,
Where shadows dance and giggles flow.
In every rustle, there's humor found,
In the twilight's magic, joy abounds.

## Stories Nestled in Felted Moss

Nestled deep where soft moss grows,
The stories bloom, as laughter flows.
A snail tells tales of daring dreams,
While birds chirp round in giggling schemes.

A toad recites his princely lore,
As butterflies twirl and beg for more.
The whispers of grass join in the fun,
With secrets shared from sun to sun.

A wise old tree scratches its bark,
With every creak, it leaves a mark.
The squirrels gather, ears aglow,
As if they're waiting for the show.

So lean in close, and hear the cheer,
In mossy nooks, the sound is clear.
With every tale, the forest spins,
A tapestry of chuckles and grins.

## Twilight's Song Among the Boughs

At twilight's door, the laughter rings,
As shadows dance on playful wings.
A fox jokes with a passing deer,
While fireflies light the evening sphere.

The brook hums low a bubbly tune,
While frogs croak out a comical swoon.
The woodpecker taps in perfect time,
Each peck a note, each echo a rhyme.

The owls are counting all the stars,
While raccoons plot their late-night bars.
Beneath the glow, the moments blend,
As woodland friends play without end.

So join in joy, let laughter flow,
In every rustle, let spirits grow.
For in this twilight symphony,
The boughs swell up with harmony.

## The Serenity of Sunlit Glades

In a glade where the sunbeams dance,
Squirrels plot their little prance.
Birds gossip about the latest scoop,
While rabbits hop, forming a troupe.

A ladybug wears a tiny hat,
Thinking it's grand, imagine that!
Bees buzz around, acting quite grand,
While flowers laugh, 'This place is a band!'

Amidst the grass, a toad's on a spree,
Trying to croak a tune, oh so free.
But all he gets is a chorus of 'ribbit',
As butterflies flutter, calling him for a visit.

Sunset glimmers, they share a joke,
Even the trees seem to poke and poke.
Under the sky, so clear and bright,
Nature's laughter fills the night.

## Tales of the Whispering Branches

The branches chatter in a soft breeze,
Telling tales with the greatest ease.
A woodpecker giggles, pecking away,
While a chipmunk grins, enjoying the play.

"Did you hear about the owl who hooted,
And scared the mouse who had just suited?"
The branches shake with laughter anew,
As shadows dance and the stories brew.

A raccoon stumbles, caught in a snack,
With crumbs on his chin, he can't take it back.
A squirrel jokes, "You should share your fries!"
While the leaves rustle with muffled sighs.

As twilight settles, the secrets unfold,
In this woodland realm, there's laughter retold.
Every branch whispers, each leaf joins the fun,
Nature's humor shines bright as the sun.

## The Hidden Harmony of Nature

In the forest, a harmony plays,
With critters dancing in their own ways.
A hedgehog waltzes, quills held high,
While a frog croaks in a tie and bow tie.

A raccoon conducts with a stick in his hand,
As raindrops fall like a beat from a band.
The snails move slow, keeping perfect time,
While ants march in, forming a rhyme.

The daisies stretch, trying to sing,
While a dragonfly swirls, doing its thing.
"Let's make a choir!" the grasshopper said,
"Just mind the cat, or you'd end up dead!"

Chirps and giggles, a jolly old tune,
Nature's own symphony under the moon.
In this hidden realm, laughter resounds,
In a joyful harmony, happiness abounds.

## Beneath the Hushed Crowns

Beneath the crowns of green and brown,
Squirrels wear leaves like a royal gown.
A rabbit debates on fashion and style,
While a turtle thinks, "I'll stay for a while."

A fox in slippers sneaks through the grass,
With a grin that says, "I'll let nothing pass!"
Trees giggle as the shadows creep,
While ants in line are counting sheep.

The owls hoot loudly, sharing a plot,
While a deer munches, lost in thought.
"Did you hear about last night's fun?"
As laughter echoes, they bask in the sun.

In this quiet nook, they share a big laugh,
Where the fun-loving critters all share their path.
Under their crowns, in peace they dwell,
With stories so funny, they ring like a bell.

## In the Company of Timeless Trees

In the shade, we sit and chat,
Old trees listen, what of that?
They've seen it all, the joy, the strife,
Yet still they stand, a tree-ish life.

Squirrels in suits scurry about,
Ranking acorns, there's no doubt!
A wooden lawyer gives a gavel,
"Let the nutcases here unravel!"

Birds tweet gossip, it's quite a scene,
Spilling secrets in shades of green.
With roots so deep, they can't be miffed,
While we all laugh, they just drift.

So raise a glass to the leafy crowd,
They give us shade and laugh out loud.
In the company of timeless trees,
Life is a joke, and nature's the tease.

## A Chorus of Bark and Bud

The chorus sings, oh what a sight,
Bark belts high, and buds take flight.
A comical tree tries to dance,
Wobbling limbs in a leafy prance.

Branches crack jokes in the evening light,
"Why don't trees tell secrets at night?"
"Because they always leaf a trail,
And squirrels just follow without fail!"

The flowers giggle, they can't hold tight,
Budded laughter, pure delight.
Each rustle tickles, a breezy jest,
Nature's humor is truly the best.

In this forest, the fun won't cease,
With every whisper, we find our peace.
A chorus blooms in the playful glade,
Where laughter and leaves in harmony trade.

## Nature's Gentle Resilience

Look at those branches, sturdy and wise,
They poke through storms, and laugh at the skies.
As winds whirl like a wild dance,
The trees just chuckle, "Give it a chance!"

The roots shake hands with the rocks so bold,
"This weather's nothing, if truth be told!"
A sunny day, and life's as it seems,
Yet rain always follows, with squishy dreams.

Butterflies flutter, all colors on deck,
Spinning tales, what the heck?
"Why did the leaf get kicked from the tree?
He was a little too green, you see!"

So here in nature, we find a smile,
Through laughs and giggles, let's pause for a while.
With gentle resilience, trees stand tall,
In their leafy laughter, we are all enthralled.

## The Lament of the Lost Sapling

Once was a sapling, eager to grow,
But tripped on a root, oh no, oh no!
"Life's a tall tale," it sighed with a pout,
"Under this leafy cloud, I want out!"

It watched big trees sway and jest,
While it was stuck in a tangled mess.
"Why can't I climb beyond this mound?
While they spread their limbs, I'm stuck on the ground!"

The wise old oak chuckled nearby,
"Patience, young sprout, don't rush to fly!
You'll need a good pruner for fashion's sake,
Or you'll look like toast after a bad bake!"

So the little sapling tried its best,
Waiting for nature, it joined the jest.
With roots so deep, it learned to sway,
Life's funny chapters can brighten the day.

## **Whispers in the Canopy**

Squirrels debate just what to wear,
Acorns tumble without a care.
Birds gossip in humorous tones,
While spiders weave their webs like phones.

A raccoon steals a picnic treat,
While the sun bakes a frog's two feet.
The branches sway and share a joke,
As turtles giggle, starting to poke.

What's that noise? A laughter spills,
The trees join in with gentle thrills.
Nature's comedy show starts on cue,
With punchlines flying like leaves do too.

## Shadows of Ancient Boughs

Underneath the mighty shade,
A snail holds court, quite unimpressed.
Critters gather, plans are laid,
For a dance-off that never rests.

A wise old owl with glasses thick,
Claims he can outsmart a stick.
The shadows chuckle, join the throng,
As the leaves sway to the silly song.

With each gust, laughter sparks anew,
The squirrels giggle with raucous crew.
The ancient boughs lean in to hear,
A gossip session, loud and clear.

## **Leaves of Time's Embrace**

Frogs in tuxedos leap and spin,
While ants debate on who will win.
A leaf drops down, a joker sly,
Mimicking a bird, it flutters high.

The sun peeks through in fits of glee,
As shadows dance, oh what a spree!
Nature's pulse in perfect beat,
With laughter tipping on its feet.

A breeze whispers tales of the past,
Of mischief played and friendships vast.
So every leaf has a story told,
In the light that sparkles, bright and bold.

## Secrets Beneath the Bark

What secrets do the trees confide?
A chipmunk winks and bumps with pride.
Beneath the bark, some riddles fester,
As mushrooms giggle, ready to jest.

The wind teases the roots below,
Tickling tales of woe and glow.
While squirrels plan a prank or two,
In the shade, where laughter's true.

Is that a whisper, or just a sway?
Nature's humor keeps boredom at bay.
The laughter bubbles, a joyous spark,
In the hidden realm beneath the bark.

## The Forest's Lament

In the shade of grand old trees,
Squirrels plan their nutty schemes,
With acorns tossed like flying pies,
They giggle as they dodge the bees.

Moss carpets all, like green confetti,
While frogs leap in a dance so petty,
A woodpecker's three-part joke,
Makes every nearby critter unsteady.

The owls hoot in rhythmic cheer,
Mocking the deer who slip in fear,
But roots weave tales of tangled fate,
In the forest, laughter's always near.

So, raise a branch, let stories flow,
About the antics only they know,
While leaves rustle with knowing delight,
The woodland crew steals the show.

## Songs of the Elder Trees

Under the canopy, secrets collide,
The wise old trees chuckle inside,
Sharing stories of squirrels as jesters,
With their nutty tricks, quite the ride.

A raccoon prances in with flair,
Wearing a crown made of fresh air,
He claims to rule all twigs and roots,
While the owls in hoots declare.

Beneath the stars, bark band plays loud,
Caterpillars form a groovy crowd,
Twisting and turning with shiny wings,
Joining in fun, nature's proud.

As moonlight glimmers through the trees,
The woodlands dance at gentle ease,
In this merry haven of laughter,
Anthems of joy sweep with the breeze.

## **Treetop Reveries**

High above, where the giggles squawk,
Birds narrate tales in cheerful talk,
Branches sway while the critters cheer,
Nature's stage, the trees unlock.

A mischievous raccoon steals the show,
With acorns launching, oh what a throw!
Each splash of laughter echoes bright,
As squirrels argue on who's the pro.

The sun peeks through in warm surprise,
Lighting up the mischief in their eyes,
As leaves rustle like a crowd in awe,
And every creature plays and flies.

So let them play, these woodland pals,
Inventing games that tickle and douse,
In treetop dreams where laughter reigns,
And puppet shadows dance like owls.

## Murmurs of the Woodland

Soft whispers float through leafy glades,
Where giggles mold in playful shades,
The hedgehogs roll in their bubbling laughter,
In this nursery where escapades are made.

A baby bird with a wobbly try,
Flies high then lands with a silly sigh,
The raccoons clap, rolling on the floor,
Poking fun at the awkward flyby.

Mushrooms nod as if in on the play,
While rabbits hop and dance away,
In this realm where every sound,
Is a tickling nudge to brighten the day.

So let the echoes spread like glee,
And nature grin where all are free,
In this woodland laughter's bounty,
Where every moment's pure jubilee.

## Songs of Lost Seasons

Once I lost my favorite hat,
It flew away, what of that?
A squirrel snickered, quite bemused,
As I chased it, quite confused.

Fallen pine cones roll with glee,
Whispering secrets to the bee.
A raccoon giggles, oh so sly,
And steals my sandwich as I cry.

The autumn dance brings wacky sights,
Leaves in costumes, oh what delights!
Frogs in tuxedos sing a tune,
While I ponder, did I miss the moon?

Summer fades, the air grows chill,
The trees conspire with a thrill.
I trip on roots, let out a yelp,
And blame the trees, they must've felt.

## The Symphony of Leaves

In the forest, branches sway,
Leaves play music, come and play.
A toad joins in, a mash-up tune,
Squirrels dancing 'neath the moon.

The oak's a maestro, proud and grand,
Bowing down, it makes its stand.
The wind joins in, a breezy friend,
On this concert, there's no end.

Raccoons tap dance on the ground,
A catchy beat all around.
Chipmunks laugh, they join the fun,
In this leafy jam, we've all won!

With each rustle, a joke they tell,
Nature's giggles ring so well.
Life's a melody, light and bright,
As trees sway on this funny night.

## Beneath the Moonlit Arbor

Under branches, shadows creep,
Whispers of the woods, they leap.
A fox in glasses reads a book,
While owls scandalously look.

The moon is laughing, round and fat,
"Who's making noise?" asks the cat.
A possum juggles acorns, bold,
With talent that's a sight to behold.

Twinkling stars join in the fun,
As critters play 'til day is done.
A dance-off starts, who'll take the prize?
The trees are judging with wise eyes.

We'll banter till the first light gleams,
Sharing silly, crazy dreams.
The forest echoes with our glee,
Who knew nature could be this funny?

## A Tangle of Branches

Branches twist in a funny spree,
Limbs outstretched, just wait and see.
A squirrel attempts a high dive,
And lands with flair, oh how he thrives!

The vines are gossiping, so sly,
As ants parade in suits, oh my!
A bulbous beetle rolls on through,
It's a circus, who knew it too?

A woodpecker's drum rings loud and clear,
As I giggle, shedding a tear.
The forest shimmies with such flair,
Who thought nature was a comedy fair?

Leaves toss tales to pass the night,
A caper here, a joke in flight.
In this tangled world, fun prevails,
As laughter dances on the trails.

## **Rhythms of the Quiet Grove**

The squirrels hold a dance-off,
Chasing shadows, oh what a scene!
They twirl and leap with much flair,
While birds chirp tunes, quite serene.

A rabbit hops and takes a bow,
Claiming victory, what a cheek!
While turtles play their slow jam beats,
As frogs provide the croaky sneak.

The breeze joins in, a gentle tease,
Tickling leaves with laughter bright.
Each critter joins, a merry gang,
Creating joy from day to night.

When sun dips low, they strut and sway,
Underneath the twilight show,
In the quiet grove, they celebrate,
What a wild party from roots to bough!

## The Daydreams of Rustling Leaves

In the canopy, leaves chatter,
Impersonating a busy crowd.
'Who's got the best shade?' they wonder,
While sunbeams giggle, unbowed.

A nutty acorn starts a tale,
Of brave adventures, climb and swoop.
The ghosts of branches steal the show,
With silly pranks, oh what a troupe!

The breeze whispers, 'Let's take a nap,'
But instead they burst into fits.
Daydreaming of far-off lands,
Where laughter never quite quite quits.

As twilight casts a drowsy shroud,
They yawn and stretch, the show goes dim.
But in the night, under the stars,
Their chuckles echo, a soft hymn.

## Spirits of the Age-Old Forest

In the heart of the ancient woods,
Spirits frolic in moonlit haze.
With tricks aplenty and playful glee,
They whisper secrets through the maze.

One ghostly figure flips a twig,
Turns it into a flying wand.
The owls hoot, they can't believe,
As shadows waltz across the pond.

They gather at the roots for fun,
A comedy show beneath the trees.
'Why do leaves never stop falling?'
'They've got busy lives – like bees!'

As dawn approaches, laughter swells,
Time for the spirits to retreat.
Yet echoes of their merry tricks,
Will haunt the groves, a joyous beat.

## Conversations with the Elder Oaks

The elder oaks confide in me,
With creaky voices, wise and loud.
'We've seen the silliness of folks,
And the wonders of the crowd!'

They chuckle low at clumsy deer,
Who trip on roots, all in good cheer.
The foxes strut with tails so high,
Pretending to be brave, not mere.

'Why do you take life so serious?'
They ask with leaves that rustle bright.
'The world's a stage, a giant play!'
Join us, let's dance 'til night!

The sun dips low, their tales endure,
Of laughter shared through every season.
With a wink and creak, they bid adieu,
As I wander home, heart full of reason.

## The Canvas of Nature's Breath


In the forest of giggles, where squirrels convene,
A painter named Nature, with colors unseen.
With brushes of sunlight, she dabs and she swirls,
Making landscapes of laughter and whimsical twirls.

The rabbits wear goggles, their ears laid back,
While deer in ballet shoes dance on the track.
The trees start to chuckle, their leaves in a spin,
As critters join in, with a wink and a grin.

An owl in a bowtie, oh what a delight,
Recites silly sonnets beneath the moonlight.
The stars play marbles, all twinkly and bright,
In this dazzling realm, everything feels right.

So here in this haven, where joy takes its flight,
Nature's magic unfolds, a whimsical sight.
With each whispered breeze, a chuckle we chase,
In the canvas of joy, there's no frown to face.

## Unfolding Threads of Life and Time

In the tapestry woven, where jokes intertwine,
The threads dance and shimmer, all silly and fine.
A rabbit with spectacles reads each silly rhyme,
While turtles, in top hats, keep perfect time.

The wise old owl cackles, as squirrels juggle nuts,
While ladybugs waltz, calling everyone 'chumps'.
The canvas keeps shifting, a riot of sound,
As every great creature joins laughter unbound.

The fox plays a fiddle, the raccoon holds a sign,
"Join the fun parade, oh, won't you be mine?"
With each joyful step, we each do our part,
Unraveling moments, right out of the heart.

In this realm of pure chuckles, time ticks away,
Each laugh is a thread in the fabric of play.
So let's toast with acorns, in this silly climb,
To life's funny moments, so precious, so prime.

## The Silence of Time Stood Still

In the meadow where daisies poke fun at the sun,
Time takes a pause, as if life's a pun.
The bees are debating who dances the best,
While ants in tuxedos play cards for a jest.

A fox with a feather duster cleans up the glade,
As frogs in top hats croak tunes they've made.
The old wooden bridge starts to giggle and creak,
As time stands in silence - a comical streak.

Mice toast with acorns, in champagne of dew,
While clouds overhead blend their laughter in blue.
So here in this stillness, the joyfully odd,
We find giggles galore, and it feels like a nod.

Each second a giggle, each minute a song,
In this timeless tranquility, we all belong.
So settle, take root, in this silly thrill,
And savor the moments, where laughter does fill.

## Transience Under the Arching Trees

Under the arching canopy, shadows play peek-a-boo,
With nature's oddball critters, just waiting for you.
The deer play charades, their faces a sight,
While chipmunks recite poetry, bringing sheer delight.

The wind plays the harp, and the leaves sway in tune,
As laughter erupts with the bright afternoon.
A raccoon with a monocle declares, "Let's race!"
While turtles roll by, at their own fevered pace.

With songs of the crickets, the best stand-up gig,
And owls who drop punchlines, oh, they're quite big!
So under these trees, where the weird and wild meet,
Every moment's a treasure, every laugh a sweet treat.

So let's twirl in the shadows, and dance in the light,
Celebrate transience, with laughter in sight.
For time is a jester, and we are its fans,
In the glade of the giggles, where joy never spans.

## Twilight Beneath the Sycamore

In the twilight, critters prance,
A squirrel slips, gives us a chance.
He lands where shadows start to play,
Whispers of wind laugh, "What a day!"

Beneath the branches, tales unfold,
A raccoon sings, so brave and bold.
We chuckle at this woodland show,
As fireflies twinkle in the glow.

The owl hoots a silly tune,
While frogs croak loud, 'We're here to swoon!'
Each leaf a note, the breeze a chord,
Nature's band, never ignored.

Grinning, we join the leafy cheer,
Their symphony we hold so dear.
With every giggle, every jest,
Under the sycamore, we're blessed.

## Heartbeats of the Dappled Glade

In the glade, the sunbeams play,
A rabbit hops, 'Why not ballet?'
Chipmunks strut in a tiny line,
With tiny hats, they look so fine.

The deer prance about like clowns,
Smirking through their leafy crowns.
A gentle breeze begins to tease,
Whispers a joke through swaying trees.

Bees buzz and hum, they tell a tale,
Of flowers, mischief, and a snail.
With humor ripe as fruit in bloom,
In this merry patch, we find our room.

Laughter dances with the rays,
Echoing through the golden days.
In moments sweet, we lose our fuss,
In dappled glades, we laugh with us.

## The Resounding Silence

In silence, whispers softly creep,
A turtle naps and starts to leap.
The bunnies giggle, 'What a sight!'
As loons float by, pretending flight.

A mushroom gossip, 'Did you hear?
The raccoons plan a party near!'
With funny hats made of green grass,
They'll dance till dawn, let no hour pass.

Crickets play their hidden games,
While ants march on with funny names.
In echoed hush, the laughter rings,
A silent jester, nature sings.

The quiet hum of funny pranks,
No need for words, we give our thanks.
In mellow tones, we share our cheer,
In the stillness, joy is near.

## **Roots of Memory**

Amidst the roots, old tales reside,
A frog jumps by, full of pride.
A vine wraps round like a big hug,
Nature's quilt, snug as a bug.

'What stories these old roots convey!'
Said the wise crow, in a witty way.
With cackles loud he'd kick a stone,
The echoes back would laugh and groan.

Each knot and twist a chuckle shared,
With fables spun, we've all prepared.
A giddy breeze tosses leaves around,
In ancient tales, our joy is found.

So here we sit, with friends in tow,
Amidst the rhythms of ebb and flow.
Each rooted moment a glimmer bright,
In laughter's glow, we find our light.

## Veils of Mist in the Elderwood

In shady nooks where squirrels play,
I tripped on roots, oh what a day!
The fog rolled in, bid dreams to wake,
I laughed at shadows, saw a snake.

With every whispered, leafy joke,
The trees joined in, began to poke.
An owl hooted, sharp and clear,
It seemed to say, 'Have no fear!'

But then I sneezed, and branches swayed,
An acorn dropped! I felt afraid.
The tiny critters snickered loud,
As I danced there, oh so proud.

With each misstep, the air grew light,
I spun around, a comical sight.
In mist and mirth, I found my way,
Elderwood antics made my day!

## Hushed Reverie of Forest Floors

The ground was soft, a bouncy bed,
I flopped and rolled, like joy, I said.
Mushrooms laughed, a colorful crowd,
'Get up, you fool!' they sang out loud.

With crickets playing a lively tune,
I gathered leaves, my great festoon.
A squirrel stopped to steal the show,
With dance moves that would steal a foe.

The sun peeked in, with a cheeky grin,
I joined the fun, let laughter spin.
Yet tripped on roots, and fell with style,
Even the trees erupted in guile.

So here I lay, the forest's clown,
In wonderland, I'll never frown.
For every stumble, a giggle shared,
In hushed reverie, I'm prepared!

## The Ancient Circle of Life

Beneath the boughs, where legends sprout,
I met a rabbit who looked about.
He spoke of wisdom and oddly ran,
In circles wide, like only he can.

An owl with spectacles perched so grand,
Shared tales of squirrels and their band.
The gossip spread like leaves in wind,
Humor brewed thick, as laughs rescind.

A deer walked in with a shiny crown,
Declared, 'In here, you'll never frown!'
Each critter shared their quirkiest jest,
In this grand circle, we felt blessed.

But when I tried to join their chat,
Stumbled and fell, oh, imagine that!
Laughter echoed through every bough,
In this ancient ring, I'm one of them now!

## Fables Woven in Wood and Shade

In shady groves, where stories twine,
A bear read plans for a dance divine.
With wiggly toes and a wacky hat,
He shimmied and shook, imagine that!

A fox with style, a coat so bright,
Told fables of treasure, oh what a sight!
But everything glimmered, even the mud,
As they plotted to outsmart a thud.

The wise old turtle, moving slow,
Joined in the fun; he stole the show.
With each laugh shared, the woods came alive,
Fables were woven, we all did thrive.

Yet as we danced, the moon slipped in,
And shadows giggled at my clumsy spin.
In wood and shade, fables spun free,
From laughter's heart, they bloom with glee!

## **Ballad of the Gentle Breeze**

In the glade where laughter sways,
Breezes tickle in playful ways.
Leaves dance on branches, oh so spry,
Squirrels giggling as they fly!

A gust blows hats into the air,
A dance-off starts with flair and dare.
Nature chuckles, it's quite a show,
As chipmunks join the waltzing flow.

With whispers soft and secrets shared,
The wind's a jester, truth is bared.
Branches sway with silly glee,
While daisies laugh, "Oh, look at me!"

So tip your hat, and twirl with trees,
Join the fun with the frolicking breeze.
Nature's humor, wild and free,
Echoes through this mirthful spree!

## The Heartbeat of Dappled Light

In sunlight's play, the shadows prance,
The forest floor invites a dance.
A rabbit trips on its own feet,
And mossy bank can't take the heat!

Beams flicker like a firefly,
Their winks and nudges always pry.
In this light, laughter finds its way,
As butterflies boogie, come what may.

The trees tell tales in light's embrace,
With bark-a-logs the squirrels base.
They foolishly leap from boughs so high,
Only to land with a comical sigh!

When dappled rays gleam on the ground,
A tangle of giggles can be found.
Nature's rhythm keeps hearts so bright,
In the pulse of these vibrant sights!

## Secrets Beneath the Forest Floor

Beneath the leaves, a secret giggles,
A wiggly worm has mastered wriggles.
Ants hold meetings with snacks galore,
As mushrooms share gossip, what a score!

Roots entwine like friends in jest,
Finding laughter, never rest.
In the damp, bolstered bed of loam,
The toads tell tales of their grand home.

With underground fiestas, sly and quick,
The whispers tell of a magic trick.
Earthworms twirl in wormy cheer,
While moles dig holes without a fear.

So if you kneel in the soft, dark earth,
Listen close, you'll find their mirth.
For in the quiet, all creatures know,
Life's a joke beneath the show.

## Whispers of Wind and Wilderness

When winds arise with playful cheer,
They tease the trees, and all can hear.
A swaying branch waves to and fro,
While giggling leaves say, "Go, Toro!"

In the bushes, a chattering crew,
Bunnies hopping, they're quite the view.
With every rustle, a chuckle grows,
As nature's voice warmly glows.

Birds create choruses of delight,
Cheeky melodies take their flight.
Chirping jokes on the bubbling brook,
While the plucky crickets write the book!

So heed the whispers in the wood,
Embrace the laughter, it's all good.
For amid the pines and playful glint,
The wilderness holds a hearty hint!

## Woodland Reveries Beneath the Sky

In the trees, the squirrels play,
Chasing shadows, night and day.
With acorns flying left and right,
They giggle softly, what a sight!

Amidst the branches, wise old owl,
Thinks he's cool, but what a fowl!
With beady eyes, he gives a wink,
As raccoons dance and cats all think.

Beneath the twinkle of the stars,
Turtles race with their tiny cars.
While rabbits hop with utmost glee,
You'd think they had too much green tea!

In this woodland so surreal,
Every critter's got a deal.
Be it mushroom, leaf, or vine,
They all gather for a good time!

## Echoes of Twilight in the Thicket

The hedgehogs roll like tiny balls,
While fireflies light up the halls.
The crickets sing their twilight tune,
While frogs just croak to mock the moon.

Bunnies with hats, so very dapper,
Look at them hop—oh, what a caper!
They have a ball, or maybe two,
With carrots tossed, like confetti too!

Foxes gossip, tails held high,
Plot some mischief, oh me, oh my!
As raccoons wear their masks with pride,
In this thicket, there's nowhere to hide!

With each echo through the night,
The woods keep laughing, what a sight!
Even the leaves seem to chuckle,
In this realm of night-time sparkle!

## Chronicles of the Breathing Wood

Once there was a tree named Lou,
Who snored so loud, it shook the dew.
The critters gathered, ears turned wide,
As whispers danced from side to side.

The cunning crows devised a plan,
To wake old Lou—they just ran!
With wiggly worms, they did entice,
Oh, what a ruckus! Quite the slice!

Frogs took bets- would Lou awake?
As silly snickers filled the lake.
But low and behold—he just snoozed,
While bushy tails remained amused!

Through time they told this fable grand,
Of Lou the Tree who would not stand.
In whispers sweet, they still recall,
How laughter echoed through it all!

## Between the Twists and Turns of Time

In the woods where branches sway,
Time gets lost, or so they say.
With squirrels trapped in endless chase,
They zoom around this wacky space.

The wise old turtle walks so slow,
To teach the young ones 'go with flow.'
But tiny bugs just zip right past,
In a whirlwind of fun, so fast!

There's mischief hidden in the glade,
Where shadows dance and jokes are made.
With every twist, a chuckle sounds,
As time and laughter spill the grounds!

So if you wander, take a peek,
At the wonders that woodland speaks!
With every moment that we share,
Laughter echoes everywhere!

## The Echoing Canopy's Lullaby

Beneath the trees, where whispers play,
A squirrel forgot his acorn today.
He squawks and jumps in a frantic spree,
While birds just laugh from the old oak tree.

The branches sway, in a groove so neat,
While critters compete for the best seat.
A raccoon winks, with mischief's flair,
Guess who's getting the last berry there!

The leaves gossip tales of the day's blight,
Of foxes who danced in the pale moonlight.
They chuckle and chirp, in perfect time,
Echoes resound, like a silly rhyme.

So if you wander, just take a chance,
Join in the forest's whimsical dance.
With laughter the breeze, light-hearted and spry,
The trees will giggle as you pass by.

## Gnarled Narratives of Yesteryear

The old trunk moans, with stories to share,
Of squirrels who thought they could fly through the air.
A chipmunk once claimed he could run faster,
But tripped on a root, now he's a disaster!

Leaves rustle softly, with secrets they keep,
Of owls who snore and never lose sleep.
The grass nods along, a comical sight,
While the bunnies debate, 'Who jumps higher at night?'

A knot in the bark holds a once-famous name,
Of a beetle who dreamed he could win WWF fame.
He trained with the ants, in a dust-bunny gym,
But lost in the shadows to a mighty slim whim.

So gather around, for each twist and turn,
The woods tell us tales, we never could learn.
With laughter in leaves and the sun hanging low,
Join in the stories, let your heart grow!

## When the Moonlit Leaves Sing

When night falls softly, the leaves begin,
To croon a melody, where dreams break in.
A cartoonish owl jokes, 'Who needs a song?
I've seen raccoons dance all night long!'

Beneath the moon's glow, shadows take flight,
As crickets are tuning, oh what a sight!
The fireflies flicker in a rhythm of glee,
While the night air giggles, so carefree.

A fox steals a glance, with a mischievous grin,
Planning a dance-off to see who will win.
The treetops shake hands, with branches that sway,
Inviting us all for a jubilant play.

So listen closely to the chorus of night,
Where laughter and song make everything right.
In this quirky forest, fun never ends,
With moonlit leaves where joy transcends.

## **Guardians of Heartwood Secrets**

In a furry old nook, the wise ones reside,
Guardians of laughter, with giggles like tide.
The hedgehog with spectacles reads from a book,
Of pinecone adventures, come take a look!

The wise old woodpecker taps out a tune,
While the rabbits do jigs by the light of the moon.
Secrets are whispered, in a quiet retreat,
About pine sap pop and the best candy beet!

A badger once plotted to steal some cake,
But tripped on a twig and fell in the lake.
His friends all rolled over, laughter in tow,
As he shook off the water, putting on a show.

So tread through the wood, with a smile on your face,
For jesters and jest are the heart of this place.
While guarding the secrets of heartwood delight,
The spirits of laughter embrace every night.

## **Whispers of Forgotten Trails**

In the woods where lost socks hide,
Squirrels giggle, they won't abide.
Every twig tells a silly tale,
Of disco frogs and a snail that flails.

Under leaves, the whispers grow,
Of gnomes with hats too big to show.
Jumping jacks done by a tree,
As owls laugh in a chorus, whee!

Mushrooms wear polka dots so bold,
Bouncing beetles like marbles rolled.
They dance beneath the crescent moon,
As crickets chirp a wacky tune.

A fox in boots starts to prance,
Inviting all to join the dance.
So many chuckles hide in the trails,
Where nature's humor never fails.

## The Craft of Nature's Breath

Breezes whisper jokes to each flower,
As bees buzz by with a sense of power.
A spider knits with threads so fine,
While beetles line up for the next big shine!

Rabbits juggling carrots in the park,
While turtles race—their shells leave a mark.
The breeze tickles leaves, starts a chatter,
Every sound is sweet, nothing's the matter.

There's a squirrel with a penchant for pranks,
Stealing hats from the riverbanks.
Mice put on shows beneath the trees,
With acorns as props, they aim to please!

Boys and girls wander here and there,
Laughing at antics—without a care.
Nature's got a humor so divine,
You'll burst with laughter—every time!

## Dusk Among the Stalwarts

As the sun dips low and the shadows stretch,
The trees start to gossip, you can bet.
A hedgehog stands guard, but oh what a sight,
He's wearing a hat, what a curious plight!

Owls hoot jokes from their lofty perches,
As fireflies flash with their bright little searches.
Bats flit about, stylish in flight,
In leather jackets, oh what a night!

Frogs croak tunes, a band they create,
With rhythmic ribbits that can't wait.
The moon starts to chuckle, with a grin so wide,
As laughter of creatures dance side by side.

"Who's wearing the funniest shoes?" they call,
A raccoon laughs, "They're my winter haul!"
In dusk's light, silliness finds its way,
Amongst stalwarts, it loves to play.

## Echoes Through the Thicket

In thickets dense where giggles grow,
Bunnies hop with a twinkle, oh so slow.
Chasing their shadows, they trip and fall,
"Who put that rock there?"—laughter calls!

The breeze carries whispers of silly feats,
As daisies twirl in their dancing beats.
A parrot squawks jokes from a nearby branch,
While ants form a line for a grand food ranch.

There's a raccoon with a questionable stash,
Collecting shiny things in a flash.
With every echo from the tangled trees,
Nature's humor spreads like a gentle breeze.

In this thicket, laughter never dies,
The world seems funnier through brightened eyes.
So join the chorus, let merriment ring,
In this playful sanctuary, where jesters sing.

## Veils of the Verdant Past.

In a forest deep, I found a shoe,
It smelled of cheese, but it danced like new.
Trees giggled softly, leaves in a whirl,
As squirrels debated, who'd take the twirl.

A mushroom wore glasses, quite the sight,
Claimed wisdom from fungi, shone in moonlight.
The winds retold jokes from years long gone,
While chipmunks freestyled, the forest was won.

A tree stump acted, as if it were king,
With a crown made of acorns, it ruled everything.
Birds chirped of deadlines, nuts must be stored,
In the midst of laughter, who kept their hoard?

With laughter echoing down every lane,
The forest became an odd comedy train.
As night fell gently, we danced in delight,
The verdant past whispered, "Let's party all night!"

## Whispers of the Woodland

In the hush of the night, the owls would hoot,
While rabbits recited the tales of the root.
The mushrooms were mulling, full of delight,
Planning a party to end all the night.

A fox dressed in plaid, oh what a sight,
Offered his jokes, they landed just right.
The badger composed, a song for the crowd,
And the trees clapped along, kind of loud and proud.

The stars twinkled bright, like laughter unchained,
While fireflies buzzed, their dance uncontained.
A raccoon with flair stole a cap from a crow,
"Turned fortune to laughter, now watch me glow!"

By the creek, the fish, they leaped with a splash,
Challenged the beetles, a rhythmic clash.
In whispers of woodland, mischief revealed,
Even shadows in giggles, their fate was sealed.

## Shadows Beneath Ancient Canopies

Beneath the vast shadows, a cat took a seat,
Proudly declaring, "I'm light on my feet!"
A squirrel chimed in, "You're more of a flop,
With your fluffy ambitions, you'll never stop!"

The brook gurgled laughter, a ticklish sound,
As turtles debated who'd swim 'round and 'round.
A pigeon quipped jokes, perched high on a bough,
"Why did the chicken? Oh! No one knows how!"

The trees held their breath, each branch a delight,
As shadows danced freely, in the pale moonlight.
With each silly quip, the night came alive,
Ancient canopies grooved, and the critters would thrive.

In the heart of the night, mischief took flight,
As dreams spun 'round, making laughter take height.
The shadows were merry, the forest aglow,
In whispers of joy, the moon said, "Let's go!"

## The Leaf's Quiet Confession

A leaf on the ground, wrote tales in the dust,
Of winds that once giggled, leave stories in trust.
It whispered to acorns, afloat in their dreams,
"Remember the summer? The rips and the seams?"

With chuckles of breezes, a twig swayed along,
"Your stories are quirky, but don't get me wrong.
I'll take my own turn, and twirl through the day,
As long as the sunlight continues to play."

Beneath a stout oak, where shadows convene,
Creatures gathered 'round, forming quite the scene.
A caterpillar giggled, "I'll dance like a star!"
The leaf added, "Sure, but do it from afar!"

The sun set in hues of orange and red,
"Join me in laughter," the leaf lightly said.
With each little rustle, echoes did blend,
In a lively confession, where fun had no end!

www.ingramcontent.com/pod-product-compliance
Lightning Source LLC
Chambersburg PA
CBHW070751220426
43209CB00083B/397